Catherine of Siena

A Simply Saints Book

Kathy Donlan

dedicated to my parents in gratitude
for my fabulous name

Introduction

Catherine and I haven't always been BFFs. Actually, when I began learning about my patron saint, I was a little disappointed. I really enjoy hearing about saints who have to struggle, at least a little. I identify with Teresa of Avila who loved parties, fine clothing and rich foods before she reformed the Carmelites. Even Therese of Lisieux, the Little Flower, had to be cured of sensitivity one Christmas. Catherine just always seemed to have it together. Like that girl who sat in front of me in <u>eighth grade</u> <u>science</u>: <u>smart, funny, holy, pretty</u>:

I've never been able to stand those sorts of people!

Catherine of Siena

It wasn't until a couple of years ago that I started praying to Catherine for help with my prayer life, and **boy did she come through.** I could really feel her presence and her love and her hope that I could know Jesus as she does, as a real friend and the spouse of her soul. I began talking to Jesus as a friend. Prayer came easier and more often than in the past. The saints became more real to me, and I could feel their presence in my life.

Now Catherine is one of my best friends in Heaven. I go to her all the time with problems big and small.

1347-1360

Catherine

Catherine was the 24th child of Lapa and Giacomo Benincasa, though some of her siblings didn't survive into adulthood (this was a time before vitamins, fluoride toothpaste and regular bathing). Even so, she had a ton of brothers and sisters. And on top of that, the house in Siena was always full of in-laws, cousins, grandparents and friends who would come to stay for long periods of time.

For a little girl who only ever wanted quiet time with God, she handled this household chaos exceptionally well. This makes her the perfect person to pray to when you just want your family to leave you alone! In fact, Catherine was so bright and merry that her family gave her the pet name Euphrosyne which means joy. So when I pray to her I like to call her Syne, because only real friends use nicknames.

Catherine was always a pretty devout little girl. One of her favorite prayers was the Hail Mary - coincidentally, that's also one of mine. When she was six she had a vision that made her long for time with Jesus even more.

She and her brother Stefano were walking home after visiting their sister. Catherine stopped in the middle of the street, but her brother - completely oblivious - kept walking. Eventually he noticed that he was alone. He figured she would be along soon. Stefano was used to Catherine stopping to pray at odd times.

When several minutes passed, he walked back to where she was and took her hand. She burst into tears. She had been looking at Christ, risen and seated on His throne, with Peter, Paul and John standing near.

Her oaf of a brother had completely ruined the vision — and I thought my brother was annoying he never ruined any of my visions, I can tell you that. Of course, I never had any . . .

Anyway, this is one of the many times in this book where a cartoon isn't going to cut it, but I gotta try.

Whelp, I was right. The cartoon didn't do it justice, but you kind of get the idea. After the vision Catherine only ever wanted to pray, do penance and teach others to pray and do penance. Her friends loved to join in her fun. The group of them made shrines and held solemn processions. They made little sacrifices and composed new prayers.

When Catherine was seven she made a promise to never marry, but to live only for Jesus.

1360-1364

Catherine's mom, Lapa, didn't know about this vow, but she would find out. When Catherine was twelve Lapa began trying to find her a husband. People got married a lot younger back then, and Catherine was so lively and attractive that it seemed like a good idea. Lapa dressed Catherine in bright dresses and jewels,

An older sister gave Catherine beauty advice. And everyone introduced Catherine, with a wink and a nudge, to every unmarried man they knew.

Catherine went along with these changes in her appearance out of obedience to her mom, but she changed the subject whenever marriage came up. This confused everyone, even her father Giacomo, though he was a very prayerful man himself. Back then, in Siena, young women either married or entered a convent. Catherine wasn't interested in doing either.

This was madness!

The family doubled their efforts to find a husband for their confused, youngest girl.

There are two times when a person can and actually should disobey their parents. And I'm not talking about bed time and homework time. You should disobey your parents only when they tell you to sin or when they forbid you to follow your vocation. Your vocation is God's plan for your life, and you will be much happier if you follow it. For instance, does God want you to marry, enter a convent, become a priest, etcetera? Catherine knew that God had etcetera in mind when he made her, and she stood firm.

By the way, it's a very good idea to pray to Jesus and Mary every night to help you know your vocation. Some people say three Hail Marys, but even a simple "God, I want to do your will; please show me my vocation," will do.

Catherine of Siena

Lapa kept fussing over Catherine and searching out potential husbands. It was pretty clear she wasn't going to stop until something drastic happened. So Catherine did something drastic. This was before salons and beauty products. It was a time when women grew their hair as long as they could and wrapped it in elaborate styles around their heads. And Catherine's hair was considered by all to be her most beautiful characteristic.

Raise your hand if you like Catherine's hair!

One day Catherine took her beautiful auburn hair and cut it off.

This is Catherine giving herself one of the world's first pixie cuts

Now there was no denying it. Catherine was not getting married. Lapa was furious.

Okay, for a long time I thought Lapa was a terrible person. Of course, I had my own "terrible" mom when I was a teenager, and I totally understood how bad it was for Catherine -- actually, my mom's pretty much a saint but I couldn't see that until I grew up. Here's the truth about Lapa. She wasn't terrible. She simply lived on a completely different planet from her daughter. Lapa knew that little girls grew up and got married and this made them happy. Some girls might enter a convent and that might make them happy, but no one refused to do either of these. Because if they did, **how would they be happy?** Lapa thought Catherine was being obstinate and perhaps a little bit crazy.

Another reason for Lapa's determination was that Siena was not a safe place. There were no police and few enforceable laws. One way to keep your belongings safe was to have lots of strong sons and sons-in-law around. That way, when crooks stole your things the men in your family could get them back.

Lapa decided that if Catherine would not serve the family by marrying, she would serve the family by actually "serving" the family.

Catherine became a slave in her own home. She did the chores for the entire household and wasn't even given a place of her own to sleep.

She didn't mind the chores much at all. The thing she did mind was not having time for prayer. But Catherine soon figured out how to make her work a prayer. She would pretend that her brothers and her father were the apostles and Jesus. Sometimes it was pretty easy.

Catherine, clean and gut these fish we just caught.

These two could easily be James and John.

This guy could be Peter! How?

Another way that Catherine was able to pray while she worked was to create a little cell or room in her heart. She could always go inside this room and talk to God, even when doing the most demanding physical tasks.

I'm not sure how Catherine made the cell inside her heart, but this is one way. Sr. Maura, CK, taught me this method when I was in fifth grade.

Make Your Own Heart Room

1) Imagine a heart. It can look like a valentine; or, if you are more of a science type, it can be anatomical.

2) Imagine a door in the heart. In fifth grade I imagined a purple door with a pink sparkly heart in the center, but many people prefer a simple wooden door or garden gate.

3) Pretend that you are walking through the door into a room. What color are the walls? Is there anything on the walls or around the edges of the room. The walls in my room are pink, and there is a large roaring fire in a big brick fireplace. I know some people who put pictures of their loved ones on the walls, so they will remember to pray for them. Others put olive trees in the room to remind them of Christ's agony in the garden of Gethsemane.

4) Now imagine a chair in the middle of the room. This has to be a large chair so that there is room for you and Jesus. You can sit on his lap or next to him, but the chair has to accommodate you both. I made my chair pink with sparkly purple flowers on it. You can sort of guess at the kind of fifth-grader I was. Many people picture a cozy chair from their house, a simple wooden chair or even a large rock like the one Jesus prayed on in Gethsemane.

5) Pretend you are sitting with Jesus on the chair. Talk to Him, listen or just be with Him.

I still use my heart room when I am having trouble praying. Every time I enter, I have to smile a little because I haven't ever bothered redecorating.

Now this may seem like playing pretend, and part of it is imaginary, but not all of it. Jesus really does wait for you to come talk to him. He is in your heart, closer to you than you are to yourself. You can use your imagination to help you find and listen to him there.

***

It was during her time of service to her family that Catherine had a dream about Saint Dominic. In the dream Dominic presented her with the habit of his order - the Order of Preachers - and told her that she would soon wear it.

Catherine wanted nothing more than to enter the Dominican Third Order. People who enter a third order follow a rule of life, like a monk or a nun, but remain at home. They don't take vows of poverty, chastity and obedience, so they can marry and have families. In Siena in the 14th Century Third Order Dominicans wore the Dominican habit. In fact, they were called the Mantellate because of the habit they wore. They were also typically widows or older married women, so it was a great shock to everyone when Catherine wanted to join.

1364-1367

It was Catherine's father who, at last, realized that Catherine could not be pressured to change her mind about marriage. He ordered everyone in the family to leave her to do as she pleased. What pleased Catherine was to live in a little room under the house. Here she prayed and preformed acts of penance, leaving only to go to church.

In her little room Catherine talked to Jesus like we talk to our friends. He sometimes appeared with his mother or other saints. She dearly loved the saints and not only prayed to them, but heard and saw them. She considered Mary Magdalene her special patron, and she was so enamored with Paul that she couldn't say his name without smiling. Dominic and Thomas Aquinas often visited Catherine's little room.

There was a Dominican monastery near the Benincasa house. Catherine, who knew the monastery schedule, would stay awake when the monks went to sleep, keeping Jesus company until the monks woke for their morning prayers.

Catherine begged her mom to obtain permission for her to join the Dominican Third Order. Lapa went a couple of times and asked the Mantellate to consider letting her daughter join. The women of the order said no. Catherine was too young. She might attract attention because of her beauty.

Then Catherine became seriously ill. Her skin turned puffy and discolored. She begged her mother to go again and plead with the Mantellate. Lapa feared that her daughter was on her death bed and tearfully begged the women to reconsider. Finally, she was able to persuade four members of the order to come and talk with Catherine. These four were quite impressed by Catherine's sincerity and wisdom. And no one could say she was beautiful now with her skin in this sickly condition.

They agreed to receive her into the order, but decided that they would wait until she was feeling better for her reception: a beautiful ceremony when she would be given the habit. Catherine was impatient for the reception and she prayed to the Holy Spirit, telling Him about her wish to become a Mantellate soon. Within a day she recovered her strength and her beauty. Her wait was over. She received the habit. **She was a Mantellate.**

Catherine spent her days in blissful conversation with God. But things in the little room under the Benincasa house were not always easy. At first Catherine was concerned she might not be able to tell the difference between Jesus and the devil. She knew that the devil could appear as an angel of light to trick people. Jesus told Catherine a very simple way to determine whether a vision was from Him or the devil.

Jesus	The devil
You may be frightened at first, but by the end of the vision you will be at peace.	You feel happy and peaceful at first, but after he leaves, you become afraid and your peace is gone.
This vision makes you humble.	This vision makes you prideful.
Jesus asks you to obey His Church.	The devil asks you to disobey the church and those in authority.

Often, the demons who visited Catherine didn't bother pretending to be good. They would just be their slimy old selves and tempt her terribly. One time it got so bad that she complained to Jesus, asking where he was while she was being tempted.

> He replied, "I was in your heart. I have seen how you have battled and I have assisted you."

It was in her little room that Catherine learned to read. She wanted to pray the Divine Office - a prayer that priests, nuns and many lay people say several times a day. This prayer is mostly made up of psalms and is said all over the world. If you are interested, and have a smartphone or tablet, there are several free apps that help with praying the Office.

Catherine studied the alphabet for several weeks until she decided to just ask God to teach her. One morning she told God that if He wanted her to recite the Divine Office He would have to teach her to read, because she had failed on her own. If he didn't want her to read she was fine with that too, but she wasn't going to waste any more time trying to learn to read by herself.

By the time Catherine finished the prayer she could read anything quickly and accurately.

Now this is not a good way to study for tests. But it is a perfectly fine to ask Catherine to pray that you do not waste time but learn the important material quickly. Then you have to actually study.

Catherine got herself a breviary - a book containing the Divine Office - since tablets and smartphones were not invented yet.

On Mardi Gras in 1366 the entire town of Siena was celebrating with a carnival and a feast. Catherine remained in her cell to pray for those celebrating Fat Tuesday. It was on this night that Lapa finally got her wish, Catherine was married.

And what a wedding!

Mary appeared, attended by several of Catherine's favorite saints, including Dominic and David who played his harp for the occasion. The Blessed Mother took Catherine's hand and placed it in Jesus' infant hand. The Divine Child gave Catherine a ring decorated with four precious pearls with a beautiful diamond in the center.

Then Jesus said, "Behold, I have espoused you to me."

Sigh!

Simply Saints

1367

For three years Catherine rarely left her cell or spoke to anyone but Jesus. At the end of this period Jesus let her know that it was time to leave the little room and begin her mission. He told her to start with a family dinner. She went upstairs to sit down and eat with her family, which she hadn't done in years.

May I join you?

Now that she was prepared by her three years of prayer and penance, Catherine went out to do spiritual and corporal works of mercy. She visited prisoners, nursed the sick and instructed the ignorant. She asked her father for an allowance that she could give to people in need.

He told her to take whatever she wanted, even if it meant giving away his entire house.

Catherine would leave the house each morning with food and money that she placed secretly in the houses of starving widows or poor families.

One day a beggar on the street asked Catherine for money. Since she had nothing, she asked him to come back to her house, where she would give him anything he needed. He said no, that he needed the money now. Catherine had a little silver cross on her rosary, and without hesitating she broke the cord and handed the cross to to the beggar who took it to sell.

Catherine of Siena

That night Jesus appeared to her holding her cross, but it was all covered with jewels. Jesus said,

"Daughter, do you recognize this cross?"

She replied, "Yes, but it was not so beautiful when it belonged to me."

Then he gave her the cross back with all the jewels still on it!

Lapa, who was trying to be a good homemaker, had trouble with Catherine giving away their goods. She convinced a priest to tell Catherine to stop taking from her family to give to the poor. Lapa knew that her daughter would not disobey a priest, and she was right. Catherine did stop taking money for a time, unless there was a dire need. Instead, she worked hard to show charity to her family.

When Lapa's maid was terribly ill, Catherine not only took over her duties but faithfully nursed her back to health.

Catherine was a wonderful nurse. She tried to help the worst cases, the people no one else wanted to touch. One of her patients, a woman named Cecca, was so sick with leprosy that the doctors were going to move her outside the city, so she wouldn't infect anyone else. Catherine promised to nurse the woman by herself, so no one else would have to be near her. Brave Catherine would bathe, feed and hug Cecca, completely unafraid of the disease.

Cecca was not an easy person to like. She was horrible to Catherine, accusing her of gossiping and doing her work poorly. Catherine always smiled and apologized for her shortcomings. Lapa was filled with righteous anger for Catherine. She said that if Cecca didn't like her, then Catherine should

leave that awful woman to her fate!

Isn't it a beautiful day?

No! You're late and lazy ...and stupid!.

Sorry about that. Here, let me get you a pillow.

Of course, Catherine did not abandon Cecca to her fate. Eventually the wounds of leprosy began to form on Catherine's hands, and still Catherine nursed Cecca every day. The woman died in Catherine's arms and, since no one else would touch her, Catherine buried her by herself. After this the leprosy disappeared from Catherine's hands.

A group of people began to gather around Catherine. She saw them as her spiritual family. They followed and hoped to learn from her.

Catherine was an awesome teacher.

She didn't try to make people into copies of herself but helped them become holy in their own ways. For instance, Catherine fasted every day. But when she saw that too much fasting was physically harming one of her spiritual children, she told her to fast only on Saturdays and only when she was feeling healthy.

So many people joined Catherine that two priests were assigned to follow her, so they could hear the confessions of the people she converted. I like to think of myself as a present day member of Catherine's spiritual family. I pray that she will make me a saint.

Catherine taught all those who came to her, but she never considered herself better than anyone. Jesus himself had taught her how to view sinners with deep and holy compassion, to pray for them and to say,

"Today it is you who are in the power of evil; tomorrow it will be I myself, if Divine Grace does not preserve me."

Though their main work was penance and prayer, Catherine and her spiritual family were not sour or depressed. On the contrary, joy and peace was the hallmark of their group; for as Catherine said,

> "Every step of the way to Heaven is Heaven."

This makes sense because only God can make us truly happy. Why is it so easy to forget this when Ash Wednesday comes around?

Catherine had many good friends but one of the best was her sister-in-law Lisa. Lisa would step in for her when Catherine was overcome by prayer. Once, while the women were working in the kitchen Catherine went into ecstasy. When Catherine was in ecstasy she could only see Jesus and everything else disappeared.

Catherine had stood right in the cooking fire and Lisa was sure she was horribly burnt. But Jesus protected her. She was just fine.

1368

One day Catherine's father became deathly ill and it was clear he was dying. Catherine, who couldn't bear to think of him suffering in purgatory, begged Jesus to take him straight to Heaven. He told her that, though Giacomo was a very holy man, he would have to spend a short time in purgatory before he was ready. So Catherine begged Jesus to leave her father on earth until he was ready for Heaven. This was also impossible.

Finally, Catherine asked Jesus to let her suffer in the place of her father. Jesus allowed this, but he told Catherine that she would be in physical pain for the rest of her life. She thanked him with happy tears and ran to tell her dad that he would go straight to Heaven.

Giacomo died after Catherine finished talking with him.

At the exact moment of his death Catherine felt a sharp pain in her side.

The pain stayed with her until the end of her life, and she never complained, but thought about it with gratitude and love.

1370

Lapa's health declined after Giacomo died. In 1370, she was very near death. She loved many things on earth more than she loved God, and so she was terrified to die. Catherine begged her mom to accept her death with grace, but Lapa begged her daughter to pray for a cure and
not to mention death!

While Catherine was praying, her mother actually died! Two friends, who were taking care of Lapa, told Catherine the sad news. They waited for the saint to finish her prayer before preparing the body for burial. Catherine ran crying to Jesus and told Him that she would not leave Him alone until He brought her mother back to life. She reminded Jesus that He had promised to take her family to Heaven, and she was sure her mom wasn't ready yet. Slowly, as Catherine was praying, the color returned to Lapa's cheeks, and she began breathing. Eventually she sat up and was **very** grateful to her daughter for the prayers.

Catherine of Siena

Catherine sometimes prayed for herself. It was her constant desire to grow in holiness, so she prayed the beautiful prayer, "Take my heart, Lord, and give me yours."

One day Jesus actually did this.

He came to her and took out her heart. Then he left with it. For two days Catherine could feel the hole left by her missing heart. When Jesus returned he held a brilliant, fiery heart which he placed in her chest.

She was elated and walked on air for days, asking everyone if they noticed that she was an entirely new person. No one really noticed, because she had always been saintly. But to Catherine the difference between loving with all her heart and loving with Christ's heart was profound.

Many things about Catherine are difficult for me to understand, but perhaps the most confusing is her fasting. Catherine had extreme difficulty eating anything except the Eucharist.

She said that the Eucharist and the presence of God was so nourishing that she could never desire to eat anything else.

People criticized Catherine, saying that even Jesus, who was God, ate and drank. Though it was very painful for her to chew and swallow, Catherine tried to eat a little at each meal. She did this so people wouldn't be scandalized by her.

Once a priest friend saw how difficult it was for her to eat and told her that she should stop. The little food she was able to keep down wasn't enough to sustain life anyway; she was clearly living by some supernatural grace. Catherine told her friend that she would keep eating so that others would not be scandalized any more by her and also as a way to do penance for those who commit the sin of gluttony.

It would be sinful to imitate Catherine by refusing all food. Unlike Catherine, we need food to live. But it is comforting and inspiring to know that, when I do eat too much, Catherine has done penance for me. And when days of fasting like Good Friday come around,

I like to ask Catherine to help me be filled with the presence of God rather than all the food I usually eat.

The one food Catherine longed for was the Eucharist. She lived at a time when people were not encouraged to receive the Eucharist daily. She would think we are incredibly lucky to be able to receive Jesus twice a day if we want.

When she did receive Communion, Catherine often had visions and ecstasies.

Sometimes she saw Jesus as a baby or beautiful child in the arms of the priest. Sometimes she saw the priest enveloped in flames of love or the angels holding torches around the host.

After receiving communion, she was so wrapped up in Jesus' love that her friends had a difficult time getting her attention hours later.

Catherine's care for sinners is legendary, and it makes her a great patron for anyone who ever sins. In Siena there was a rich man named Andrea de Bellanti. He didn't pray or go to church. He drank and gambled a lot, and people say he couldn't speak without swearing. While he lay dieing his parish priest went to visit him and was so scared by his blasphemy and profanity that he ran from the house. Later one of Catherine's friends, Father Tommaso, went to him. Father Tommaso would not be bullied. He stayed for three days enduring cussing and rants against God and the Church. Father Tomasso wasn't getting anywhere with the man, so he asked his friend Catherine to pray for Andrea. She did, and as she was praying Andrea yelled for his wife to get the priest.

He said that Jesus was standing in his bedroom, demanding that he make his confession. Standing next to Jesus was "that girl called Catherine."

Andrea not only made a good confession, but he rewrote his will so that his wealth was distributed to the poor and the church as well as his family. After doing this he died in peace.

Father Tommaso left Andrea's house unable to believe what just happened. He went to tell Catherine, but she surprised him by telling him all about Andrea, whom she had never met, and his house, where she had never been.

1371

Alessia Saracini was probably Catherine's closest earthly friend after her sister, Lisa. Alessia's father-in-law, Francesco, was 80 years old. He had only gone to confession once in his life and had never received communion.

Alessia hoped Francesco would get ready for Heaven by growing closer to Jesus. She invited her friend Catherine to stay with them hoping she could convince Francesco to go to confession and church. Catherine stayed all winter. Each evening Alessia, her husband, her father-in-law and Catherine would sit in a comfortable room and talk.

Whenever Catherine spoke about God, Francesco made fun of her. In fact he mocked just about everything she had to say about anything. But Catherine was her sweet, kind, clever self, and Francesco began to warm up to her. After a few weeks he was listening to what Catherine had to say. And in time he told her that he would do whatever she told him to do.

Francesco told Catherine about an enemy of his. A priest in Siena had done something to hurt Francesco. **He was so upset that he spent quite a bit of time plotting to kill this priest.** Catherine reminded the old man about the line in the Our Father – "forgive us our trespasses as we forgive those who trespass against us." She told him that he would be forgiven with the same amount of forgiveness he gave to others.

The next morning Francesco took his favorite hunting falcon and went to find his enemy. When the priest saw him coming he ran. Francesco sent another priest to tell him to come back so they could make their peace. When his enemy priest saw that Francesco was unarmed he came to meet him, with several of his friends along for support. Francesco said, "The grace of God has touched my heart. I am come to offer to be reconciled to you; and to prove my sincerity I ask you to accept this falcon, of which I am very fond." The priest accepted the gift and peace was made.

Catherine of Siena

Francesco ran back to Catherine and asked what he should do next.
Catherine sent him to confession. After avoiding the sacrament of reconciliation for decades, Francesco's confession took **three days!**

Day One
- It has been at least 60 years since my last confession.
- This may take a while.

Day Two
- Then I stole two pears and an apple from Neri.
- Wow! He's got a really good memory.

Day Three
- I'm sorry for these and any sins I may have forgotten ...father?
- Zzz zzz

While Catherine was staying with Alessia and her family, two criminals were paraded through the streets on the way to their execution. Alessia called Catherine over to the window to watch them pass. The men were being tortured as part of their punishment, but only Catherine could see the demons who were gleefully joining the torturers.

The two men refused to see a priest or pray at all. They cursed against God all the way to their death. Catherine begged Jesus to save these men. The demons were so frightened of Catherine that they came straight to her and threatened to posses her. They said her torment would be much worse than what the two sinful men had suffered. She replied with confidence, "Whatever God wills, I will."

Catherine of Siena

When the group arrived at the scaffold to hang the men, Jesus was already there. Only the two sinners could see Him as He offered them forgiveness, if they would ask for it. The two criminals asked for a priest and confessed before their death. They stepped up to the hangman as happily as if he was taking them to a party.

1373

For several years the Virgin Mary had promised to send Catherine a priest who would guide her and help her grow in holiness more than anyone had ever done. The moment she met Raymond of Capua Catherine knew he was the one Mary had told her about. Raymond became one of Catherine's best friends. When she died he wrote a touching and very long book about her. Father Raymond was pretty intelligent and Catherine always said he taught her a lot, but he insisted that it was Catherine who taught him.

Raymond did his best to make sure Catherine could receive Communion more frequently. Though she still wasn't able to receive the Eucharist daily, she was able to receive more often.

As Catherine drew more people to her with her holiness she also made several enemies. Jealous people called Catherine all sorts of names and accused her of receiving favors from the devil rather than from God.

They got so mad about her long ecstasies after Communion that some people would pick her up while she was praying and throw her out of the church.

Catherine complained to Jesus as we would to our friends, though probably with much more charity and forgiveness. Then Jesus held out two crowns: one shining with jewels and the other made of piercing thorns. He said, "My daughter, you must wear both of these. Choose now which you will wear in this life."

She held out her hand for the crown of thorns and Jesus pressed it on to her head. For a long while she felt the thorns piercing her, though the crown, like her wedding ring, was invisible to others.

1374

A fierce plague raged through Siena in 1374. This was one of the worst cases of disease. One third of the population died. Lapa Benincasa lost many grandchildren, two sons and a daughter.

Catherine, Father Raymond and her other followers nursed the sick. They comforted the dying and buried the dead. After a long day of tending to plague victims Father Raymond woke to find his hands swollen and his body burning with fever. He knew the symptoms of the plague and realized he would soon die. When morning came, he went straight to Catherine's house. She was already out tending the sick, so Lapa put him in a bed and sent someone to fetch her daughter. When Catherine returned and saw him suffering, she placed her hand on his forehead and prayed. During the prayer Father Raymond felt something violent move through him. He thought he was going to throw up. Most plague victims did that before they died. Then he felt whatever was moving in him leave through his hands and feet. Catherine looked up from her prayer, confident that he was going to be fine. She gave him some food and told him to sleep.

When he woke he was healed.

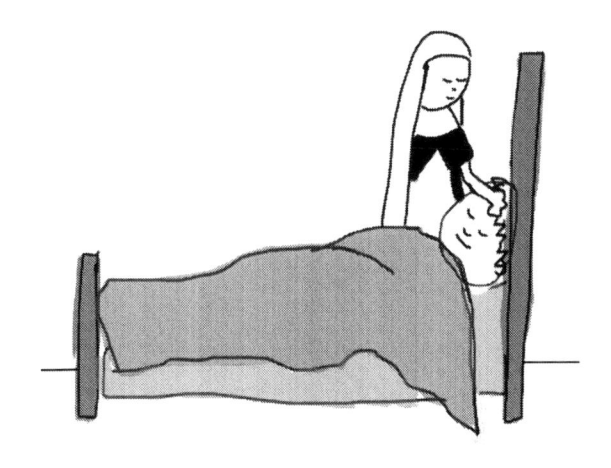

Catherine's reputation spread and many people asked for her prayers and efforts on their behalf. Lords and princes begged her to make their subjects like them and to settle disagreements with their enemies. She worked on problems for convents in Pisa and Montepulciano. She loved going to Montepulciano because the incorrupt body of Saint Agnes was kept there. One day she laid her head on the silk covering Agnes' face and sighed happily, "Do you not see the gift that Heaven sends us?"

Even Pope Gregory XI sent a cardinal to beg Catherine to pray for him. Catherine prayed, but also wrote letters to the pope, princes, abbots and abbesses, and ordinary people (well, she dictated them. Jesus had taught her to read, but not to write). These letters are beautiful statements full of courage and light. Reading them is like listening to Catherine talk right to you. Even when she writes to Pope Gregory, her desire for him to grow in holiness is so universal and so personal that you can imagine some of her sentences are written to you.

1375

Catherine was invited to Pisa to teach the nuns at a convent there. After she received Communion one morning her soul wanted to go to God so badly that it lifted her body off the ground. Then five red rays shot from the crucifix in front her. She felt the wounds of the stigmata on her hands, her feet and in her side.

The stigmata is a gift that Jesus gives to some of His saints. The person who receives this gift experiences the wounds of Crucifixion in her own body. St. Francis of Assisi received the stigmata and so did Saint Padre Pio.

Realizing what was happening Catherine begged Jesus to make the wounds invisible. She didn't want to draw any more attention to herself. Immediately the rays turned from red to white. Catherine would feel the pain all her life, but the wounds would be invisible until she died.

There was a Carthusian monastery about 20 miles from Pisa. The prior there had been a fan of Catherine's for a long time. He invited her and her friends to the monastery and put them all up in a little house. Early in the morning after they arrived he brought all his monks to the house and asked her to give them a speech. At first she refused, but then relented and spoke about overcoming temptation. The prior said that she hit the nail on the head.

It was as if she had heard all the brothers' confessions. That was how well she knew them and their struggles.

Before leaving Pisa, Catherine spoke with the leaders of the town. Florence had declared war against the pope and demanded that Pisa join them. Catherine urged the men of Pisa to ignore Florence and stay loyal to the pope. The leaders of Pisa listened to Catherine and did as she said.

Catherine of Siena

Catherine returned to Siena for a few days before receiving a letter from Pope Gregory XI asking her to go to Lucca. The city, like Pisa, was being bullied by Florence into revolting against the pope.

While she was in Lucca, a priest decided to test her. He brought her Communion, since she was sick in bed. But instead of bringing the Body and Blood of Jesus, he brought an unconsecrated host. Others in her room knelt and crossed themselves when he entered with the host, but she refused. When he scolded her for irreverence, she scolded him for causing her friends to commit idolatry by worshipping an unconsecrated piece of bread. The priest went away remorseful and with new respect for Catherine.

When she was certain that Lucca was firmly allied with the pope, Catherine left, but she kept up correspondence with leaders in Lucca and Pisa, encouraging them to stay strong.

1376

Catherine was not afraid to tell the pope and his priests what she thought. She wrote openly to Gregory XI that his cardinals, who demanded tithes from poor people, and his own indecision were the cause of the revolts around Italy

At this time the pope, Bishop of Rome, was living in Avignon. Though Gregory often spoke about his desire to return to Rome ,he never found the strength to leave the French cardinals, who wanted to keep him near. Meanwhile Gregory hired cardinals to fulfill his duties in Rome. Many of these cardinals were greedy and ruthless. They took too much money and punished those who couldn't pay. Catherine often wrote to the pope that he needed to return to Rome and stop this period of delay.

Catherine of Siena

Early in April, Jesus appeared to Catherine and placed the cross on her shoulders and an olive branch in her hand. Her mission would bring peace and hope, but **it would not be easy!**

In June, Catherine went to Avignon to meet with the pope in person. A delegation from Florence was on its way and the pope asked Catherine to make peace between him and them.

The people from Florence ignored her and left without settling their dispute with the pope. After this the French cardinals began to doubt if Catherine was really as holy as everyone said, though Pope Gregory never doubted. Three high ranking priests came to him and asked about Catherine:

Priests: Is this Catherine of Siena as saintly as she pretends to be?

Gregory: I am persuaded that she is a saint.

Priests: With your permission we will pay her a visit.

Gregory: In that case I have no doubt that you will be greatly edified.

The priests went to Catherine's house early the next morning. They told her straight out, "We are astonished that a little insignificant woman like you should presume to confer with the Holy Father on these great matters."

Catherine of Siena

Catherine received them with charm and humility. They questioned her about her visions and ecstasies, and she answered all their questions. After their interview they told the pope,

"She explained things to us more clearly and precisely than any Doctor could have done. We have never met a soul so humble and so enlightening."

Catherine didn't leave France until she was sure the pope was ready to return to Rome. Even then, she had to send him a letter from Genoa encouraging him to get a move on.

When Pope Gregory finally arrived in Italy his cardinals brought him reports of people rioting in Rome. This worried Gregory. He wondered if he should just go back to France. Then the pope remembered that Catherine was staying nearby in Genoa offering advice to all who came to her. Gregory didn't want people to see him asking for help, so he disguised himself and showed up at her house.

Catherine was able to convince the pope that moving back to Rome was the right thing to do, and Gregory continued on his way to the Eternal City.

Catherine and her spiritual family went to Pisa. They were greeted by the now elderly Lapa, who had trekked all the way there to see her daughter. Lapa was now a Mantellate, and though she didn't long for Heaven as naturally as her daughter did, she was growing in holiness in her plodding, faltering way.

In Pisa, Catherine spent some time talking to the ambassadors from Florence and from the pope, trying again to make peace between them. After several weeks of effort Catherine left for Siena.

Back home she resumed her old duties: guiding her spiritual family, caring for the sick, making peace between people and admonishing sinners.

1377

Niccolo di Toldi was scheduled for beheading for speaking against the government. He had not been to confession since his first communion, and he refused to see a priest before death. Catherine visited Niccolo the morning before his execution and begged him to confess to a priest. He said he would, if Catherine promised to stand with him when God judged him. She consented, and he made a good confession.

Early the next morning Catherine visited Niccolo and took him to mass. Then she talked with him, telling him to, "be of good cheer, Sweet Brother, for soon we shall be at the Marriage Feast Eternal." Then she went and waited for him at the place of execution.

As she waited Catherine prayed to God, Mary and Saint Catherine of Alexandria for Niccolo's soul. When Niccolo arrived and saw her he smiled and knelt down meekly. Catherine held his head as the executioner brought down the ax. Then Catherine looked up and saw Jesus taking Nicollo to Himself. She marveled at the Divine Mercy.

Father Raymond was very concerned about making sure Catherine got the Eucharist almost daily. Late one night Catherine and her group arrived at Father Raymond's monastery. Her friends convinced her that they shouldn't wake Father Raymond to say Mass for them. Catherine agreed and sent the priest a message that she wouldn't need him to say a Mass that night. Raymond had been waiting to say his Mass until Catherine arrived, so when he got the message he took out his Mass kit and said a quick Mass in a small chapel. Catherine meanwhile prayed in the main chapel.

During the Mass a piece of a consecrated host fell from the ciborium. Raymond quickly searched for it. When he didn't find it, he continued with his Mass. After the Mass he did a thorough search of the chapel. He was very distressed about losing this piece of the Sacred Host.

Raymond thought Catherine was at home, so he rushed to her house to ask what to do. Perhaps God would show her where the host was. He was surprised when Lapa told him Catherine was at the monastery. He ran back and found her in ecstasy. Father Raymond and Catherine's friends did all they could to rouse her. After several minutes the ecstasy was over. Then Father Raymond told her about his Mass and how he had lost part of one of the consecrated hosts.

Catherine just smiled as he was talking. Then Father Raymond started smiling, "Mother," he said, "I am starting to believe you know where my host is?"

Catherine nodded. Raymond asked if she took the host. Catherine shook her head. Finally Raymond ordered her under obedience to tell him what happened to the piece of host. She replied that Jesus came to her carrying it in His hands.

Jesus Himself had given her Communion that night.

No one was surprised about this. The members of Catherine's spiritual family had often seen the host fly from Father Raymond's hands to Catherine's mouth.

The demons were not happy to have Catherine back in Siena. Once, while she was traveling on a donkey with the Dominicans, the animal bucked her off. She laughed and said, "Oh that's just Satan." After she got back on the donkey it threw her again, this time falling on her. She laughed this off as well, but the monks would not let her ride any more.

Gregory called Catherine to Florence to make peace between him and the Florentines. While she was in the city, Gregory died and Urban VI was elected.

People in Florence criticized Catherine. They said that it was improper for a young lady to travel with priests and young men. They said that it was inconceivable that the pope had chosen such a young and ignorant ambassador. There were even attempts on Catherine's life.

After many months of talking to the leaders of the city, Catherine convinced a delegation to set out to Rome and ask for peace. She wrote several letters to Urban begging him to make peace. Urban did this and the delegation returned bearing an olive branch from the pope.

The Florentines celebrated.

1378

Once peace was made Catherine returned home and dictated her beautiful book. Her Dialogue is a conversation between the soul and God. I can never read it too many times.

My favorite line, and it's hard to pick just one, is this:

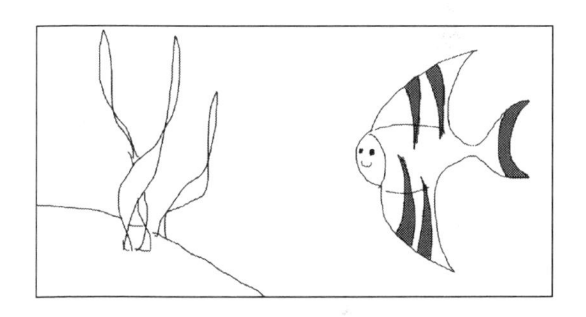

The soul is in God and God is in the soul, just as the fish is in the sea and the sea is in the fish.

It explains the life-sustaining closeness of God to the soul so very well.

During this time, Catherine kept up her intensive letter writing. She wrote to the ever-increasing members of her spiritual family, to lords and princes, and to the pope. She told Pope Urban to be more gentle with his cardinals and the people. Urban had trouble controlling his rash temper, but he tried to do as Catherine asked. He even ordered her to come to Rome and advise him. She went, with her large family including Alessia. Lapa, or Nonna (Granny) as Catherine's family called her, followed later.

Shortly after they arrived in Rome Urban sent Raymond to Bologna as Master-General of the Dominican friars there. Raymond writes that there were tears in Catherine's eyes when he left. She told him that they would not see each other again in this life. Raymond hoped that for once Catherine was wrong, but she wasn't.

1380

In the last months of her life Catherine was unable to eat or drink anything. She heard Mass daily and prayed Vespers in the church. On the third Sunday in Lent she became bedridden. Her suffering increased, but she remained joyful, always thanking God for His "fresh proofs of love."

In April, when she could tell she was going to die, Catherine gathered her spiritual family and gave them some parting advice about how to grow in holiness. She told them that they were truly her family and she was their mother, that in Heaven they would be her glory, her crown, and that she would pray for them in Heaven. She commanded her family to pray for the Church and the pope.

Then she called them one by one and told them what they should do after her death. After this, she asked pardon for all the times she was not a perfect example of good works and virtue.

Next she made her confession and received Communion. She could no longer speak, but breathed gently. A priest gave her the last rites. An hour and a half later she said, "Lord have mercy on my words." She repeated this about 60 times. She was resting on Alessia's shoulder and she tried to get up, but couldn't. She gazed at the crucifix and begged mercy for her many sins.

Last, she made the sign of the cross, blessing her little family. She said, "Yes, Lord, You called me and I go to You! I go, not because of my merits, but of your mercy; and I implore that mercy in the name of your most Precious Blood. Father, into your hands I commend my spirit." And she died.

The stigmata appeared on Catherine's hands and feet. And a ring of lighter color flesh appeared on Catherine's ring finger.

That same morning, miles away Father Raymond was praying before an image of the Virgin Mary. Suddenly, he heard the words, "Fear not! I am here for your sake! I am in Heaven for you. I will protect and defend you. Be at peace, and fear nothing, for I am here for you!" At first Raymond thought Mary was speaking to him, but that didn't make sense. He went through all the possibilities in his mind until he realized it was Catherine, and he knew she had died.

Catherine was canonized a saint in 1461. In 1866 she was proclaimed one of the two principal patrons of Italy along with Saint Francis of Assisi. In 1970 Pope Paul VI proclaimed her a Doctor of the Church.

Knowing Catherine's love for each soul she encountered, it is not very far-fetched to imagine her talking to you:

"I am in Heaven for you . . Be at peace and fear nothing for I am here with you."

Acknowledgments

Anyone who writes a biography of Catherine of Siena owes Blessed Raymond of Capua a debt. He wrote an exhaustive, beautiful biography that I used as my major source.

I am also grateful to Sigrid Undset for her well written biography of the saint.

EWTN's webpage about Catherine was invaluable for quickly checking dates or the order of events.

My husband, Michael, was a very patient editor. Sister Mary Angela, CK, also lent her editing talents to this project. I can't thank them enough.

About the Author:

Kathy Donlan teaches resource and special ed. CCD at St. Joseph Elementary School in Lincoln, NE. She is a wife and mother to three active boys. In her limited spare time she cartoons pictures of saints, writes about saints, reads about saints and plays video games.
She can be contacted at kdonlan@hotmail.com.

Printed in Great Britain
by Amazon